SACRAMENTO PUBLIC LIBRARY

828 "I" Street

Sacramento, CA   95814

4/10

TH
LONDON BUS

James Tay

D1007835

SHIRE PUBLICATIONS

First published in Great Britain in 2009 by Shire Publications Ltd, Midland House, West Way, Botley, Oxford OX2 0PH, United Kingdom.
443 Park Avenue South, New York, NY 10016, USA.

E-mail: shire@shirebooks.co.uk   www.shirebooks.co.uk

© 2009 James Taylor

All rights reserved. Apart from any fair dealing for the purpose of private study, research, criticism or review, as permitted under the Copyright, Designs and Patents Act, 1988, no part of this publication may be reproduced, stored in a retrieval system, or transmitted in any form or by any means, electronic, electrical, chemical, mechanical, optical, photocopying, recording or otherwise, without the prior written permission of the copyright owner. Enquiries should be addressed to the Publishers.

Every attempt has been made by the Publishers to secure the appropriate permissions for materials reproduced in this book. If there has been any oversight we will be happy to rectify the situation and a written submission should be made to the Publishers.

A CIP catalogue record for this book is available from the British Library.

Shire Library no. 499   •   ISBN-13: 978 074780 728 5

James Taylor has asserted his right under the Copyright, Designs and Patents Act, 1988, to be identified as the author of this book.

Designed by Ken Vail Graphic Design, Cambridge, UK and typeset in Perpetua and Gill Sans.
Printed in Malta by Gutenberg Press.

09 10 11 12 13   10 9 8 7 6 5 4 3 2 1

COVER IMAGE
The archetypal London double-decker, an RT-type AEC Regent, pictured in Whitehall when new in 1950.

TITLE PAGE IMAGE
A London bus conductor punches a ticket for a lady passenger. Artwork taken from a London Transport poster of 1947.

CONTENTS PAGE IMAGE
London's routes were numbered from the earliest times, and the buses carried destination indicators – initially boards, later roller blinds like this one – to help would-be passengers.

ACKNOWLEDGEMENTS
Photographs and illustrations are from the author's collection except as follows, acknowledged with many thanks, and where copyright is reserved: Imperial War Museum (IWM), pages 34 and 42; London Transport Museum, front cover and pages 1, 4, 6 (bottom), 11, 12 (bottom), 14, 15 (top), 16, 18, 19 (top), 20, 21 (bottom), 23, 24, 26, 27, 28 (both), 29, 30, 31, 32, 35 (both), 36, 37 (bottom), 44, 47, 48, 49, 53 (top), 54 (top), 56, 57, and 60 (both); Graham Smith, pages 3, 6 (top), 7 (bottom), 8 (bottom), 9 (bottom), 10 (both), 15 (bottom), 21 (top), 22, 33, 37 (top), 40 (top), 50, 52 (middle and bottom), 55 (bottom), 58, 59, 61 (both), and 62 (bottom); Mike Sutcliffe, MBE, pages 13, 19 (bottom), and 38; and Phil Wilson, page 39.

Shire Publications is supporting the Woodland Trust, the UK's leading woodland conservation charity, by funding the dedication of trees.

CONTENTS

The London Double-Decker

'B' Type Motor Bus
The first London General standardised motor bus, first introduced in 1910. It had a petrol engine and seats for 34 passengers. Its design was so successful that 2,900 were built and the last vehicle in the type was not withdrawn from regular service in London until 13 October 1926. Over 1,000 saw war service in France, and General's in those days were the B's. The B14–18 war. Unladen weight 3 tons 11½ cwt.

LUT Trolleybus No.1 – 'Diddler'
London's first trolleybus, which operated from 16 May 1931 until 1948. It came out of retirement in 1962, when it carried dignitaries on the last day of trolleybus operation in London. Capacity 56 seats. Unladen weight 8 tons 2 cwt.

'ST' Type Bus
This most all reliable bus first appeared in 1929, and 1,140 were built. The six-cylinder engine was a 6-cylinder overhead camshaft petrol unit. London had 3 ST which were fitted pneumatic tyres with covered tops. These represented the finest design available. Between 1932. These were the first buses equipped with a covered cab. Registered and ST type in petrol-engined vehicles throughout their working life for about 10 years. It saw competition at the war years between 1942 to 1944 as a make-do job. These buses had the war which returned the bus without the double decking and under the type was stationed by a body buildings, and vehicles. The ST remained in service until 1950. Capacity 48 seats. Unladen weight 6 tons 12 cwt.

'K' Type Motor Bus
This type of bus of the K class were built between 1919 and 1926. It was the first bus designed with four wheels within, which enabled the bus body itself to be constructed to the 2ft 2in width permitted by the regulations. Tramways of this first having 24 passengers, could now be fitted on either side of the gangway in the lower deck, giving the bus a carrying capacity of 46. Another innovation was a driving position placed beside the engine instead of behind it. K424 was built in 1920 and was one of the last five still in service in 1932. It remains in full working order. Unladen weight 4 tons 8 cwt.

LCC Class E1 Tramcar
Car No.1025 is one of an early series built by these under County Council between 1910 and 1922. This car was built in 1910 and modified several times. Many cars of this type remained in service with London Transport until the end of tramway operations in 1952. Capacity 73 seats. Unladen weight 18 tons 10 cwt.

'LT' Type Motor Bus
One of the earliest six wheelers, with seating for up to 60 passengers. The type was in service from 1929 until 1949, and the first 150 models without outside staircases and petrol motors. LT165 was one of the correct to be built with an enclosed staircase and was converted to diesel engines in 1938. It was withdrawn in 1949. Capacity 56 seats. Unladen weight 8 tons 5 cwt.

'NS' Type Motor Bus
This type of bus was introduced in May 1923 and incorporated a low chassis frame which was intended to allow the provision of a covered top deck. Owing to police objections, however, buses ran without covered tops until 1925. NS 1995 is in its final form, also having pneumatic tyres and an enclosed cab. It ran from 1927 to 1937. Capacity 52 seats. Unladen weight 5 tons 11½ cwt.

Printed by Impress (Acton) Ltd.

THE LONDON BUS AND ITS OWNERS

BUSES IN LONDON haven't always been red, they haven't always been double-deckers, and they haven't always been powered by internal combustion engines. Yet the archetypal London bus is all of these things. In fact, the archetypal London bus is no more, having been swept away by the tide of progress. There are still red double-deckers plying London's streets, but they are no longer owned by a single company and are no longer built to a degree of standardisation that was once the envy of bus operating companies around the world. They have even been joined by large numbers of single-deckers, which were once to be found only on low-demand routes in the outer suburbs of the metropolis. Fortunately, some of London's iconic double-deckers still run on what are called 'heritage' routes, to the delight of tourists and older Londoners alike. There are many more to be found in museums and in the hands of bus preservationists.

ORIGINS

To explain where the London double-decker came from, we have to go back to the later part of the nineteenth century, when public transport was provided by horse buses. Nearly half of these were owned by the London General Omnibus Company (LGOC, or the 'General'), which had been established in 1855.

London's first horse-bus service was opened in 1829 by George Shillibeer, who had brought the idea over from Paris. In fact, it was French entrepreneurs who, having established a thriving business by buying up most of the independent horse-bus operators in Paris, formed the LGOC by doing the same thing in London. By 1859, the Compagnie Générale des Omnibus de Londres had become wholly anglicised, but it did not have things all its own way: a number of bus operators had held out and had retained their independence.

All the early horse buses were single-deckers, but before long their operators began to look for ways of packing more passengers into them. Without a major increase in size, the only way was to provide seats on the roof of the bus, stagecoach fashion, and so the double-decker was born.

Opposite: London has seen double-decker trams and trolleybuses as well as double-decker buses. This poster, issued in 1977, shows (clockwise from top left) a 1911 B-type, a 1931 trolleybus, an NS-type from the 1920s, an LT-type six-wheeler from the 1930s, a typical tram, and ST-type from the 1930s and (centre) a K-type dating from 1920.

One operator that had not given in to the General was the London Road Car Company, which used the Union Jack fleet name as a direct and patriotic taunt to the General's French origins. It was Union Jack who, in the 1880s, first provided a loading platform outside the body of the bus and gave its 'outside' (top deck) passengers a proper staircase. As others copied these innovations, the basic shape of the double-decker bus was established.

Above:
Not every London double-decker has been red: this Routemaster double-decker was specially repainted for the Shop-Linker service in the 1980s, which linked the shopping meccas of Knightsbridge, Regent Street and Oxford Street.

Right:
London buses have traditionally had a fleet number consisting of a type designation and a serial number. The fleet number seen here, RT4712, is on the bonnet of an RT-type, the largest of London's standardised classes.

Left to right:
The Bell Punch
tickets shown here
date from the late
1960s and early
1970s. Next to them
are earlier punch-
type tickets, dating
from the days of the
LPTB. The two maps,
from 1960 and 1979,
helped passengers to
decipher London's
confusing bus
network.

The traditional
London bus stop –
in this case a
'request' type (you
had to signal the
driver) rather than
the 'compulsory'
type, which had a
red logo on a white
background. The
lower segment
was usually filled
with metal plates
indicating which
routes served
the stop.

MERGERS

Nevertheless, there were no motor buses in London before 1899, and no
really reliable ones before 1904. These early vehicles were in effect motorised
horse-buses, and their bodywork reflected the fact. Extreme caution by the
Metropolitan Police Public Carriage Office, which licensed buses to run on
London's streets, held back the design of the motor bus for many years but
could not prevent its proliferation. By 1908 there were over a thousand
running in the capital, and within two years the General, at
least, would cease horse-bus operation and go over entirely
to motor buses.

After a particularly bad year in 1907, the three largest
London bus operators – General, Union Jack and Vanguard –
realised there was too much competition and decided to
join forces under the LGOC name. On their amalgamation
in 1908, they owned 885 of the 1,066 buses then in service
in London. The General's red livery (adopted in 1899
– then a more sombre crimson than the vermilion used
later) thus became the dominant one in London.

However, buses were not London's only form of public
transport, and a major player was the Underground group,
which operated a large part of the 'tube' or underground
railways. In 1912, fearing competition from the rapidly increasing numbers
of motor buses, Underground bid for and absorbed the LGOC, which

Above:
Examples of the
E-plates or route
number indicators
used on bus stops.

nevertheless retained its name. Over the next twenty years, some of the buses owned and operated by the LGOC ran in the colours and with the fleet names of other companies bought out by Underground, but this was largely to retain passenger loyalty. Some of the independent operators remained in business for a time, and in the 1920s were joined by others who jostled for business on the General's own prime routes. It was not until 1933 that the mess was sorted out.

LONDON TRANSPORT AND LATER

Many years of discussion had led to the formation of the London Passenger Transport Board, which came into being on 1 July 1933. Parliament granted it monopoly powers to provide bus, tram, trolleybus and railway services across the whole of greater London and, with the LGOC at its core, the LPTB absorbed the buses and routes operated by over sixty other companies. The General fleet name began to disappear along with the liveries of the former independents, and London would henceforth be served by smart red buses (with white-painted areas of relief) that wore the London Transport name on their sides.

Politics brought about the next change in the operating authority. After the end of the Second World War, the Labour government led by Clement Attlee forged ahead with nationalisation, and the LPTB was nationalised as the London Transport Executive (LTE), under the control of the British Transport Commission (BTC), which took responsibility for a number of other bus operators in Great Britain, as well as for British Railways.

These three classic
London buses are
now in
preservation. The
ST-type on the left
(dating from the
1930s) and the
G-type Guy in the
middle (dating
from 1945) would
both have
belonged
to the London
Passenger
Transport Board
when new. The T-
type single-decker
on the right was
new to the LGOC,
or the General, as
its fleet name
shows.

The LTE continued the standardisation policy of its forebears, but further political changes (this time under a Conservative government) saw it renamed as the London Transport Board (LTB) on 1 January 1963 and placed under the direct control of the Minister of Transport. Just seven years later, the government handed over the management of London's buses to the Greater London Council, which had no mandate for much of the London Country Area (served by London Transport buses in green livery; see page 51) and so handed over both this and the Green Line (its express coach services) to the new National Bus Company.

In 1984, the then Conservative government took back control of London's bus network from the GLC and created London Regional Transport (LRT). With this change, London Transport became a contract tendering authority that owned the routes rather than the buses. Some dozen separate bus-operating units were formed over the next few years in pursuit of the government's privatisation aims, but all had been sold off by the mid-1990s to become private companies, dividing among themselves London's fleet of

Typical of London's more modern double-deckers is this VLA-class Volvo operated by Arriva. That fleet name was seen on buses all over the UK, but Arriva's London fleet wore the traditional red livery associated with the capital's buses.

Londoners have had to get used to a variety of fleet names since the 1980s. This TP-class Plaxton-based Dennis double-decker belonged to Metroline, whose conventional red buses were distinguished by a blue line.

London buses move into the twenty-first century with this experimental no-emissions fuel-cell Mercedes-Benz Citaro bus, which entered service in 2004. Its operators were not shy to advertise what it was!

4,600 buses. Then in 2000, LRT was replaced by a new authority, Transport for London (TfL), which was no longer state-owned but rather an arm of the newly established Greater London Authority (GLA). Once again, routes were contracted out to a variety of companies.

Although these companies mostly retained the traditional red London bus livery and mostly operated double-deckers, the impressive fleet standardisation that was once the pride of London Transport has now vanished.

EARLY HISTORY

A S THE TWENTIETH CENTURY opened, London was still wedded to the horse bus. There were 3,736 of them in the capital in 1901, of which almost half were owned by the LGOC. A motor bus had run experimentally in 1899, but the LGOC first tried one out four years later. It was a Fischer petrol-electric double-decker imported from the USA, but it was not a success and the first mechanically propelled LGOC bus that the Metropolitan Police licensed for service was a single-deck Clarkson steam bus in 1904.

London's first buses were horse-drawn. This example was pictured in 1890 in service at St John's Wood.

The LGOC tried several different types of motor bus over the next few years, as did other London operators. After its merger with Union Jack and Vanguard in 1908, the LGOC found itself with a large and motley collection,

and the directors identified a pressing need for standardisation. Their chief engineer, Frank Searle, eased the situation by re-allocating buses so that each garage ran only a small number of different types and its maintenance staff could build up the relevant expertise. He then persuaded the LGOC to manufacture its own buses to a standardised design in the large bodybuilding works it had inherited from Vanguard in the merger.

Searle himself designed the new bus to meet the latest Metropolitan Police Public Carriage Office regulations laid down in 1909, which quite savagely limited the weight of the vehicle as well as its overall dimensions and seating capacity. The first prototype of the X-type (its name will be explained later) emerged from the works at Walthamstow later that year.

Frank Searle can be seen as the father of the London motor bus. As the LGOC's chief engineer, he was the man who came up with the design of the X-type in 1909 and the even more important B-type in 1910.

The X-type used the best features and many components of existing buses. It had a straight wooden frame perched above the axles, with steel flitch-plates for strength. The driver sat behind its four-cylinder petrol engine and there was a chain-driven three-speed gearbox (the Metropolitan Police had banned the prototype's gear-driven type because it was noisy). Like existing horse buses, it had a narrow lower saloon that seated sixteen passengers in two longitudinal facing rows. There was a staircase at the back leading to a further eighteen seats on the open upper deck or 'outside'.

This 1906 De Dion is typical of the variety of vehicles that the General operated in the early days of the London motor bus.

Sixty examples were built, all in 1909, plus one lorry on the same chassis, but Searle was already improving his original design. By October 1910, he was ready with the new B-type. Although the B was very similar in appearance to the X, it had been specifically designed for volume production – the first bus ever to be so – and it made Searle's name. It was just what the LGOC needed, and by 1911 more than 1,000 were in service. A total of 2,826 had been built by the time production was suspended for the duration of the First World War, and more would be built in 1919.

In fact, the B-type was so successful that the LGOC ran its last horse bus just a year after its introduction. In that same year, 1911, Searle was poached by the Daimler company, who had him design a rival to the B-type that they

The oldest London motor bus still in existence is this 1909 Leyland X-type, not to be confused with the similarly-named LGOC X-type designed by Frank Searle. It was operated by Central, one of the independant operators allied to the LGOC.

could sell to independent operators. He went on to join the Tank Corps in the First World War, then returned to Coventry and BSA (Daimler's holding company) and later became managing director of the Rover car company. He is still celebrated as the father of the London double-decker motor bus.

The two most important factors in the design of his B-type were reliability and standardisation. Even though small numbers were built with single-decker bodies, the basic design of the bus remained unchanged. As these buses proliferated across the LGOC garages, operating and maintenance staff needed to become familiar with fewer different types of bus. They built up a body of expertise which was very much to the benefit of the LGOC, while the stocking and provision of spare parts was also simplified. It was a lesson that London's bus operators would not forget.

The names of X-type and B-type given to Searle's designs for the LGOC had not been picked at random. From 1906, the LGOC began to

The B-type bus was Frank Searle's masterpiece. Introduced in 1909, it influenced the design of double-decker buses for the next twenty years. This example, B340 dating from 1911, is now preserved in the London Transport Museum collection.

give its buses 'bonnet numbers' which identified their type. Thus the numbers 101 to 199 were reserved for those on Straker-Bussing chassis, 201 to 299 for De Dion Bouton types, and so on. This worked fine until the 1908 merger, when it became impossible to accommodate the large numbers of new buses from the Union Jack and Vanguard fleets within the numbering system.

So the LGOC devised a new system with a code letter to identify the type and a serial number after it. The Milnes-Daimler buses of different varieties became classes A, D and E; the Straker-Bussing buses became classes F and G; and so on. There were so many different types in the LGOC fleet at this stage that by the time Frank Searle's first design was ready in 1909, the next available letter was X. So the new buses were numbered X1 to X60. When his second design was ready a year or so later, many of the early buses had been withdrawn and the letters were being re-used, and so it became the B-type. This system set a precedent that has been followed by London bus operators ever since.

Meanwhile, another system of numbering had been introduced – this time for the routes on which the buses ran. The first numbered bus routes had actually been introduced in 1906 by Vanguard, but the LGOC adopted the practice and it has remained unchanged to the present day.

It was also in this period that the LGOC settled on a brighter red to distinguish its fleet from the buses of other operators in London. That colour has become so closely associated with transport in the capital that when London's buses were privatised in 1994 there was a stipulation that at least 80 per cent of the new fleets must be painted London Bus Red.

Even so, there have been variations on the livery over the years, and in this early period some LGOC buses were given brown panels below the lower-deck windows. In the period between about 1904 and 1908, some LGOC buses also ran in other colours when they shared routes with horse buses. During 1913, a few appeared in a red, white and green scheme, the green being mostly applied to the lower panels and staircases.

This 1913 poster advertises a special Sunday service. The open-top double-decker belonging to the LGOC was typical of the period.

The arrival of the motor bus in the early years of the twentieth century brought a new breed of sign to London's streets. This one was outside a bus garage.

PRIVATE

FOR QUOTATIONS
APPLY
PRIVATE HIRE DEPARTMENT
31, BROADWAY,
WESTMINSTER

GENERAL

-V.L.Danvers-

SUMMER OUTINGS
BY PRIVATE BUS

GENERAL

BETWEEN THE WARS

T HE TWO DECADES between the end of the First World War and the start of
the Second World War witnessed huge changes in the design and operation
of London's buses. Buses became more reliable; they gained pneumatic tyres,
enclosed top decks and enclosed staircases; and their operating authority
underwent a fundamental change of corporate identity in 1933. But throughout
the period, the operating authority groped steadily towards standardisation
while eagerly exploiting every concession made by the licensing authorities
towards larger buses that were capable of carrying more passengers.

The Metropolitan Police regulations in force in 1919 had been issued
ten years earlier and restricted the seating capacity, overall length, overall
width, un-laden weight and gross laden weight. Double-decker buses could
not have roofs on the top deck because the Public Carriage Office worried
that a heavily laden bus might overturn if it had to swerve to avoid an
accident. Tramcars, by contrast, ran on rails and could not swerve, so they
could have closed top decks.

It was the middle of the 1920s before the Public Carriage Office relaxed
that requirement, and the LGOC rushed to provide its new and existing
buses with roofs, although some older vehicles remained open-toppers until
they were withdrawn from service. The Public Carriage Office was also slow
to permit windscreens for the driver, and to allow enclosed staircases, but by
the end of the 1920s these anomalies had been sorted out.

Of greater concern to the LGOC than these design issues, however, was
competition from so-called 'pirate' operators. It was not until the 1930 Road
Traffic Act that routes had to be licensed, and from August 1922 the LGOC
had to put up with a number of rival companies that ran buses on the LGOC's
own routes and effectively robbed it of passengers. The competition was
sometimes good-natured: the author's mother and aunt remembered 'pirate'
buses out-manoeuvring the General's in traffic and announcing their earlier
arrival at bus stops with a cheeky toot on the horn. Arguably, the competition
was good for the LGOC in the long run, but the 'pirates' were a thorn in its
side until they were swept away by the 1930 Act of Parliament.

Opposite:
In the inter-war
years, the country
really was just a
bus-ride away from
suburban London,
and hiring a bus
for a weekend
outing must have
been a special
treat for middle-
class families.

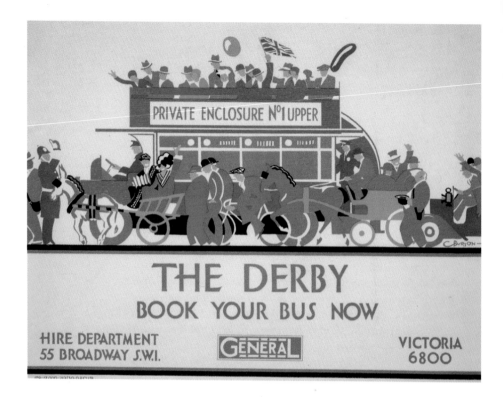

THE DERBY
BOOK YOUR BUS NOW

HIRE DEPARTMENT
55 BROADWAY S.W.I.

GENERAL

VICTORIA
6800

A few open-top buses were retained for private hire duties, such as the trip to the Derby horse races advertised on this 1930 poster. The bus was a ready-made grandstand on arrival at the race course.

In 1919, the Associated Equipment Company (AEC) resumed construction of B-type buses for the LGOC, but that same year the first of a radically new model was built. To get maximum room for passenger seating in the body, the K-type moved its driver to a position alongside the engine instead of behind it. This 'forward-control' position was matched by newly permitted increases in overall length and width. Most importantly, however, by bringing the sides of the bus out to the full width of the axles there was room for forward-facing seats in pairs on each side instead of longitudinal inward-facing benches. The result was a massive increase in seating capacity to forty-six (twenty-four 'outside' and twenty-two 'inside').

Some of the K-type buses were built as single-deckers to suit suburban routes, which demanded such vehicles, but the vast majority of the 1,132 that were built between 1919 and 1926 were double-deckers. All had a four-cylinder petrol engine that was smaller than the B-type's but just as powerful.

The S-type that came next was really an interim model, resulting from the LGOC's successful request for permission to increase the gross laden weight. Introduced at the end of 1920, when the K was still in production, it was longer overall and boasted a larger and more powerful engine. A total

The K-type gained extra passenger space by moving the driver alongside the engine. K424, seen here, was built in 1920 and now belongs to the London Transport Museum collection. It carries the later type of body with curved-under sides that was introduced in 1925, but it would originally have been straight sided.

of 928 were supplied to the LGOC and its agents, some as single-deckers.

The real change, however, came in 1923 with the NS-type. This was the first two-letter London type-code, and the LGOC claimed that it stood for 'Nulli Secundus' (second to none). The NS retained the S-type's 5.1-litre engine, but its key innovation lay in a radically new chassis design.

Up to this point, a bus chassis had been a straight frame that sat on top of the axles, giving a floor level that was high off the ground. For the NS,

The LGOC faced serious competition in the 1920s from the so-called 'pirate' operators in London. Their buses ran on the same routes as the General's, and in effect stole their passengers. This 1924 Leyland LB5 with 48-seat Dodson body belonged to the Chocolate Express company and was typical of the 'pirate' fleets.

The arrival of a covered top deck during the 1920s was a major advance in London bus design, and the NS-type was the first to have it. These examples, still on artillery-type wheels and sporting solid tyres, were pictured at Elmers End garage in 1929.

AEC's chief engineer Charles Edwards drew on American practice and designed a frame that stepped down between the axles, and was even lower at the rear to permit a low loading platform. It resulted in a bus which was nearly a foot lower overall than the S-type and considerably more stable.

The new frame demanded pressed steel construction instead of the flitched timber on earlier types, and once again the bus grew longer – to 25 feet with a 15-foot 6-inch wheelbase. Yet despite these advances the Metropolitan Police refused to approve a closed top, and so the NS remained an open-topper until the LGOC was able to win its case in 1925. The first closed bodies followed in March 1926, and many earlier NS-types were converted.

Conservative as ever, the Metropolitan Police also refused to sanction pneumatic tyres on the NS, although they were fitted to examples for operators outside London. They worried about a slight increase in overall width on the rear wheels. However, once again the LGOC pressed its case and the last of more than 2,300 NS-types for London, delivered in 1928–9, did have them.

After a brief flirtation with large-capacity six-wheelers in 1927–8 to counter six-wheelers operated by a 'pirate' company, the LGOC hatched a

The ST-type was based on the recently introduced AEC Regent chassis. Pneumatic tyres were the norm by this stage; the driver's cab was enclosed but the top deck did not project over it. This example, ST922, was delivered new in 1930 to Thomas Tilling, a major south London operator, who also built its open-staircase body. It passed into LPTB ownership when that company was formed in 1933 and is now owned by the London Bus Preservation Trust at Cobham.

The majestic LT-type six-wheelers were based on AEC Renown chassis and brought greater passenger capacity than the two-axle ST-types. This is LT165, which now belongs to the London Transport Museum and has been preserved as it would have been in wartime, with mesh over the windows, covers over the headlamps, and white-painted mudguards.

The STL was the ultimate flowering of London's inter-war double-deckers. Based on the longer-wheelbase AEC Regent chassis (hence the 'L'), it had an enclosed staircase and a full-length top deck. There were several body variations. This example dates from 1936.

plan to develop its own buses independently of AEC. However, AEC were just about to introduce a brand-new range of chassis, and early examples of these proved so good that the decision was made to remain with AEC.

London took its first examples of all three chassis in 1929. All were powered by a smooth and powerful new six-cylinder petrol engine, and their other common components had obvious appeal to the LGOC. The AEC Regal single-deckers (see page 53) became the T class; the Regent two-axle double-deckers became the ST class (the letters stood for 'short T' because the Regent chassis was a foot shorter than the Regal); and the Renown three-axle double-deckers became the LT class ('long Ts').

The ST was a remarkably robust bus. The bodywork seated fifty-two and mostly came from the Chiswick works – although there were exceptions – and a few buses to generally similar design, absorbed from other fleets, were also numbered as STs. The archetypal ST, however, had a 7.4-litre petrol engine and an enclosed-staircase body whose style quickly dated because of its projecting cab: the top deck stopped short of the front of the bus, terminating behind the line of the driver's cab.

A similar style of body was fitted to the first LT-types, but from 1932 a new and rather elegant style was introduced, where the front of the upper deck was now level with the front of the driver's cab. The maximum permitted length for a three-axle double-decker had meanwhile increased to 30 feet, and seating capacity went up from fifty-six to sixty. Early LTs had the same engine as the STs, but they soon moved to a larger and more powerful type; experiments with 'oil' (diesel) engines began in 1931, and all new deliveries from 1934 were so powered.

But further changes in the regulations governing the size of buses swiftly made both the STs and LTs redundant. As the permitted overall length of the two-axle double-decker increased yet again, AEC took advantage by introducing a larger Regent with a longer wheelbase. From 1932, the LGOC seized on this, and designed for it a new body with the latest full-length upper deck style and a more rounded, streamlined profile, which embodied the best features of their earlier designs. The new STL class ('ST long') was built to the tune of 2,701 examples, and production of the STs and LTs gradually subsided as the new bus took over. Although the first STs had petrol engines, from 1934 the LPTB decided to standardise on diesel engines because of their better fuel economy and their high torque at low speeds that was ideally suited to London traffic conditions. So, later STLs were diesel-powered.

As the 1930s drew to a close, the London bus fleet was more heavily standardised than ever before, although it still contained an entertaining mix of NS, ST, LT and STL double-decker types, plus a few oddities inherited from companies such as Tilling (which had been swallowed up by the LPTB in 1933), and some waifs and strays that had been purchased to meet shortages or for special purposes. Notable among these were the 1937 STDs, in effect STL-types on Leyland chassis but with Leyland bodywork that had been superficially 'Londonised'. Smartly turned out in its bright red livery with white around the windows and a silver roof, the London fleet was a credit to all those who worked with it as Chiswick's thoughts began to turn to another new generation of buses.

How the London bus developed (from left): a B-type, a K-type, an S-type and an open-top NS. Note how height was gradually reduced to the point where, with the NS, the Metropolitan Police Carriage Office thought the risk of a bus capsizing had been reduced to an acceptable level and sanctioned a roof for the first time.

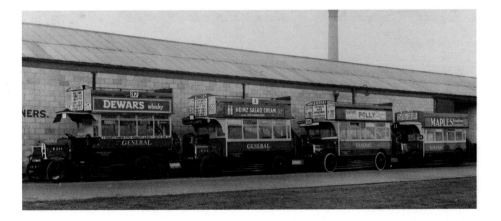

DESIGN, MANUFACTURE AND MAINTENANCE

IN THE EARLY YEARS of the twentieth century, the LGOC and other London operators tried out a wide variety of different motor bus types, many of overseas manufacture. Few were wholly reliable; some were disastrously the reverse. After 1908, when the Vanguard and Union Jack fleets merged with the LGOC, there was an even greater variety of different types for the maintenance crews to master.

It was quite clear that a reliable standardised design would make life easier for all concerned, as well as improving operating efficiency. Frank Searle, who was then the LGOC's chief engineer, deflected a management plan to buy a large quantity of Wolseley chassis and suggested instead that the LGOC should design its own buses and manufacture them at the Walthamstow works it had inherited from Vanguard.

This made perfect sense. The first LGOC design was the 1909 X-type, which was superseded by the improved and now legendary B-type in 1911. Shortly after that was introduced, the LGOC itself sold out in 1912 to the Underground group (which operated much of London's underground railway network), and its new owners saw merit in allowing the bus manufacturing operation to sell to other customers as well. So the Walthamstow works was put under the control of a new Underground subsidiary called the Associated Equipment Company, later to reach a worldwide clientele as AEC.

Even though the two were now separate businesses, AEC and the LGOC retained very close links on the design and development of new buses. It was an excellent arrangement, the LGOC feeding its considerable operating experience into the design process to the benefit of AEC products generally, and AEC being prepared to build to its largest customer's particular requirements. Although AEC became a wholly independent company in 1933 when the LGOC became the London Passenger Transport Board (LPTB), those close links remained unbroken and AEC continued to be London's first choice – although not its only one – as a supplier of buses for another thirty years or more.

Opposite: Rows of Routemasters and later DMS-type buses in the overhaul shop at Aldenham works, 1978. Note the overhead gantry crane used for moving the bodies around.

Chiswick was the
first centralised
maintenance depot
for the London
bus fleet, and here
a K-type chassis
is seen under
overhaul. The date
is between 1923
and 1925.

However, AEC – like the ex-Vanguard works at Walthamstow from which it had grown – was exclusively concerned with the chassis side of the business. Since the days of horse buses in the nineteenth century, the LGOC had maintained a bodybuilding works at North Road in London's Islington, with another nearby at Upper Street. North Road continued to build the bodies for the X-types and B-types and to mount them on chassis constructed at Walthamstow, but after the First World War it was clear that larger premises were needed.

So the LGOC decided on an ambitious and far-sighted scheme to centralise its construction, overhaul and major repair operations in one place, and in August 1921 opened a huge new engineering works at Chiswick in west London. Chiswick also became the design centre for new LGOC models, working in close liaison with AEC at Walthamstow.

Between 1922 and 1943 Chiswick also built the majority of bodies for London's buses, although some contracts were awarded to outside manufacturers when there was a need. Between 1924 and 1928, it even assembled NS-type chassis, using components delivered from AEC, but this arrangement ended when AEC moved to new and larger premises at Southall in west London. Although Chiswick remained an important element in the infrastructure supporting London's buses after the end of the Second World War, it built no more bodies because it quickly became too busy with long-overdue repairs and overhauls on buses that had worked through the war years with only minimal maintenance.

The business of regular and comprehensive bus overhaul became important very early on. From 1850, the Metropolitan Police Public Carriage

Office became responsible for overseeing the fitness for use of buses (and taxis) in London, and remained so until 1931. Not only did it lay down certain regulations – such as maximum dimensions, which constrained bus design to a degree – but it also insisted on an annual inspection. The garages of the LGOC were of course responsible for running maintenance during the motor bus era, but they were not capable of carrying out more major overhauls.

So a system was devised, in which buses due for overhaul would be driven to the LGOC's North Road works in Islington, or to a subsidiary works at Olaf Street (off the Latimer Road), where their bodies would be removed from the chassis. The chassis would then be driven back to the parent garage for a thorough mechanical overhaul, while the bodies were refurbished at the body works. The chassis would then be driven back to the body works, reunited with their bodies, and the complete vehicles would return to their operating garages. In a variant of this system used briefly during 1921, four of the larger garages were appointed as regional depots and each one dealt with all the chassis overhaul work for the smaller garages in its group.

The big change came with the opening of the Chiswick works in 1921. Garages remained responsible for running repairs and maintenance, but Chiswick became the central supplier of running spares and also became a one-stop overhaul depot. Buses due for overhaul would be driven to Chiswick, and at one end of the vast depot their bodies would be lifted from their chassis. Chassis and body then went their separate ways, through dedicated checking and overhaul shops, which broke them down into sub-assemblies (such as engines, gearboxes and axles) where necessary. Rolling

This picture gives a good idea of the hive of activity that was the Chiswick body overhaul shop in 1934. Most of the bodies seem to be from NS- or ST-type buses.

Chiswick again, and here a number of early NS-type chassis are seen on test after undergoing mechanical overhaul. The works had its own test track, complete with the dip seen here which tested the vehicles' hill-climbing ability.

chassis were reassembled and then driven and assessed on Chiswick's own test track before going back into the works to be reunited with freshly overhauled and painted bodies.

It was a brilliant system, and it produced brilliant results. When Chiswick discovered that there were often discrepancies in overhaul times (bodies generally taking longer to overhaul than chassis), this knowledge was built into the plan for the heavily standardised post-war RT-class buses. More bodies were bought than chassis, so ensuring that there was always a 'float' of overhauled bodies waiting to receive chassis as they were completed.

One interesting consequence of this system was that, in later years, a bus that emerged from Chiswick wearing the fleet number and registration

A Routemaster undergoes the famous London 'tilt test'. Packed with sandbags to represent the weight of the passengers, the vehicle would be tilted to 28 degrees from the vertical. It was of course loosely tethered to prevent disasters, but the idea was to prove that London double-deckers could remain upright in extreme conditions.

Body is lifted from chassis in the Aldenham works as the overhaul of a Routemaster begins in 1970. In fact, the Routemaster has no separate chassis – just front and rear sub-frames – but the principle is the same as it always was.

number of one that had earlier entered the works for overhaul might have no more than those two items in common with the original bus! Its chassis and body were very likely to have come from two different vehicles altogether, the great standardisation within the fleet making such hybrid creations feasible. Buses did, however, retain their own chassis and body numbers, so it was always possible for the origin of any vehicle to be determined from these.

There is no doubt that Chiswick learned the value of standardised components through its work for the Air Ministry during the Second World War. The LPTB was put in charge of the London Aircraft Production Group in 1941, and Chiswick became one of a group of London factories that produced parts of Handley Page Halifax bombers. Each member of the group built a different major sub-assembly (such as wings, fuselage, and so on), the whole coming together at the end of the process to make a complete aircraft. Without a very high degree of component standardisation, this process could not have worked. It was a lesson well learned, and it affected the whole design and operating philosophy of the RT- and RM-class buses.

Chiswick had been built in 1921 to cope with a fleet of up to 4,000 buses, a figure that seemed well out of reach then. However, by the end of the 1930s it was dealing with a fleet of 6,000, and there was every indication that this number would continue to increase. (In fact, fleet numbers peaked at around 8,000 in the 1950s and 1960s.) So after the war, when Chiswick was overwhelmed with repair work on the wartime fleet, a decision was taken to move the overhaul function to a new site at Aldenham in Hertfordshire. Originally planned as a depot for a proposed extension of the Underground's Northern Line, Aldenham had been one of the factories involved in the London Aircraft Production Group in wartime.

Throughout London Transport's heyday in the 1950s and 1960s, Aldenham therefore operated the Chiswick-developed overhaul system for London's buses, while Chiswick itself continued servicing vehicle components, retained the design offices, and was perhaps best known for its driver training 'skid pan', where new drivers were taught to control a skidding bus.

However, with changes in the ownership of London's buses, Aldenham became under-used and redundant, and closed at the end of 1986. The bus engineering for London's fleet was contracted out to Bus Engineering Ltd, who made the old Chiswick works their headquarters for a while. But, as an inevitable result of the decentralisation process initiated several years earlier, maintenance work was increasingly farmed out to operating garages. Chiswick, too, soon began to look too big and costly for the work it had to do, and in 1990 it was closed and the site was sold for redevelopment.

After the closure of the Aldenham works in 1990, maintenance and overhauls were carried out at the operating garages. This rear-engined double-decker belonging to Leaside Buses was pictured at the Wood Green garage in 1993.

LONDON'S BUSES
IN WARTIME

A T THE OUTBREAK of the First World War in 1914, the British Expeditionary Force found itself with a severe shortage of motor vehicles. Action was swift: the Army requisitioned 1,000 buses of all types from the LGOC and allocated them to the British Army Service Corps. Here, they were painted khaki and shipped across to France to serve with the BEF.

In due course, more LGOC buses would follow. They were used for a variety of purposes, although primarily as troop transports. With their windows boarded up (to guard against glass splinters) and various other modifications, each bus could carry twenty-five fully equipped soldiers. Typical uses included transport to and from the 'line' as reserve battalions replaced those who had done their turn in the trenches; many buses were also attached to casualty clearing stations, from where they evacuated the walking wounded.

Many London double-deckers were commandeered by the War Department and used to transport British and Commonwealth troops in France during the First World War. These buses are pictured transporting Indian troops behind the lines.

But not every bus remained a bus during its wartime service. There was a pressing need for lorries as well, and some buses were stripped of their bodies and converted for this purpose. At least one was turned into a mobile pigeon loft, carrier pigeons being one of the Army's favoured methods of conveying messages.

London's largest contribution was a contingent of some 900 B-type buses, of which 300 had been requisitioned as early as October 1914. Of these, a proportion returned to the LGOC and were refurbished for further service. Notable among them was B43, a 1911 example that had been among the first to go to France. Retired from active service in 1920, it was nicknamed 'Old Bill' (after Bruce Bairnsfather's wartime cartoon character), was presented to King George V, and remained an exhibition and parade favourite for many years. It is now part of the Imperial War Museum collection.

On the home front, London somehow survived without this large proportion of its fleet. Those left behind continued to ply their normal trade, although there were casualties: for example, a bomb dropped during a Zeppelin raid at the Aldwych in September 1915 severely damaged B804 and killed its driver and conductor. More of a problem was the absence of

A casualty of war: this LT-type six-wheeler is craned out of a bomb crater at Balham in October 1940. London Transport staff kept the services running in spite of the conditions.

The 'utility' bodies built during the Second World War had square-rigged lines, the aim being to minimise the need for skilled assembly workers who were needed elsewhere for the war effort. This Guy double-decker entered service in 1945.

skilled and trained men, who had been called up to fight, and from 1916 women began to take their place to keep essential services running.

The situation during the Second World War was very different indeed. This time, London had to cope with regular and severe bombing raids, and many buses were severely damaged or put beyond repair by bombs. In the early years of the war, London called for help from the provinces, and by the end of 1940 no fewer than 472 borrowed buses were working in the capital.

The biggest problem was that there were no new buses to be had. The main bus manufacturers had turned their factories over to the production of war material such as lorries and tanks, and so by late 1940 bus manufacture in Britain was at a standstill. The situation became intolerable – and not just in London – and in mid-1941 the government decided to permit bus manufacture again, but to organise it strictly so that there was minimum use of the skilled workers or scarce materials needed to support the war effort.

This scheme was overseen by the new Ministry of Supply, and it began with the manufacture of 'unfrozen' buses in 1941–2 – vehicles that had been part-built when the war halted production, or that were constructed from stocks of spares. The Ministry of Supply and the Ministry of War Transport then drew up a standard, simplified 'utility' bus specification that could be built by several manufacturers. The September 1941 prototype was built on an 'unfrozen' chassis and delivered to London after a brief spell as a demonstrator. Two chassis manufacturers were also appointed (Guy and Daimler), and although their products differed, they shared an essentially basic approach and execution. These 'utility' buses were noisy, uncomfortable and built to lower standards than those London expected.

Bus windows were often covered with mesh to protect the occupants from glass splinters if a bomb exploded nearby, but in some cases alternate windows were simply boarded up. A small hole in the mesh allowed passengers to see just enough to work out where they were during the blackout. (IWM D 2748)

By spring 1946, when its last utility-specification buses were delivered, London had been allocated 637 utility double-deckers of three major types, plus 43 'unfrozen' vehicles and a further 11 with utility bodies on 'unfrozen' chassis. It was a pitifully small number for the LPTB, which would normally have replaced its fleet at a rate of 300 or more vehicles for every one of the six years of the war. Not only were many of London's buses worn out by the end of the hostilities, but many had also received inadequate maintenance and there had of course been a number of casualties. The fleet was in desperate need of the 1,000 new RT-type buses which had been ordered in 1944 for delivery 'when circumstances permitted' – but in fact it would be 1947 before the first of these would arrive.

Meanwhile, the great London fleet struggled on. Night-time blackouts (when all lights had to be turned off or shielded to avoid aiding enemy bomber crews) meant that passengers often had to peer closely at a bus to read its destination blinds and that they could not read their newspapers in its unlit saloons.

The buses themselves had white edging painted on their front mudguards and platform edges to make them more visible in the gloom, and their headlamps were masked so that only a tiny area of light fell on the road directly in front of the bus. Many had blast netting fixed across their windows for safety, leaving just a small diamond of clear glass in the centre to help passengers see where they were.

Some of the new 'utility' buses that reached London were not painted in the capital's traditional red but rather in a red oxide colour that was the nearest equivalent then available through the Ministry of Supply. And a few buses were even converted to run on 'producer gas' (generated in a small anthracite burner towed as a trailer behind the bus) from 1941, when there were fears that Britain's oil supplies would be disrupted. By late 1944, however, the threat had receded and this highly unsatisfactory scheme was abandoned.

The Green Line coach fleet, meanwhile, had been withdrawn on the outbreak of war for immediate conversion into ambulances. This was in line with a contingency plan drawn up in 1938 which envisaged mass casualties if London were heavily bombed. Fortunately, the need for these ambulances

To overcome fuel shortages during the Second World War, many London buses were fitted with 'producer gas' trailers, which burned mainly charcoal to make a combustible gas that could be used in the engine. This one was pictured behind a later enclosed-staircase ST-type double-decker.

never materialised, and before the end of 1938 many had been re-converted for passenger use. Then as American troops began to arrive in Britain during 1942, a number were again withdrawn from service and were sent to the US Army for general transport use. Some went to the American Red Cross, and thirty-two of these were converted into mobile canteens called Clubmobiles, in which guise they saw out the war.

Welcome home: parked alongside one of its luckier comrades, which survived the war unscathed, is a former Green Line T-type coach which had seen service as a Red Cross Clubmobile with the American Forces in Britain. The picture was taken in January 1946.

ICONIC DESIGNS: THE RT AND RM

Albert 'Bill' Durrant was London Transport's chief mechanical engineer from 1933 to 1965 and the man primarily responsible for its two most iconic designs, the RT and the Routemaster.

LONDON TRANSPORT'S drive to standardise its buses reached its zenith in the two decades between 1950 and 1970 with two types of double-decker that today still symbolise the London bus right across the world. Both the RT family and the RM (Routemaster) were designed to use a maximum number of standardised, interchangeable components, and both were extremely successful types of bus that easily outlived their planned service life. It is arguable that in their essential design features they have still not been bettered for London use, although their demise came about because neither could be adapted for one-man operation when London's transport accountants demanded the change.

Both these iconic vehicles were the work of the same core design team. Project leader on the RT and RM designs was the hugely respected A. A. M. ('Bill') Durrant, who was chief mechanical engineer of London Transport's road fleet from 1933 to 1965. He was supported by J. W. Wicks, the Chiswick works manager who ran the development of the RT and led the RM body design team. Others who worked on both designs included chief draughtsman Phil Lunghi and Arthur Sainsbury, foreman of the Chiswick body shop. Only for the Routemaster did London Transport also employ an external consultant. This was industrial designer Douglas Scott, who had worked in the London office of celebrated US designer Raymond Loewy and had already designed the body and interior of the RF single-decker (see page 51). He guided the overall shape and decor of the RM, although some of his ideas had to take a back seat to the practical considerations put forward by London Transport's operational staff, and there were frequent disagreements with Eric Ottoway, Durrant's chief engineer, over the design of the body.

The RT was based on the same AEC Regent chassis as the successful STL, but with LPTB-inspired modifications. The key changes were air-operated brakes and gearbox to make the driver's life easier, and a larger-capacity diesel engine to improve acceleration in traffic. This was also detuned to reduce stresses and improve its operating life.

The first RT chassis was completed in 1938, and entered service experimentally with the open-staircase body from an older vehicle. Chiswick works completed its new body the following year to an extremely elegant design, with four large lower-deck windows, a neat fairing to blend the kerbside mudguard into the body panelling, and route number boxes at the front and rear of the roof. With an open rear platform, it seated thirty passengers upstairs and twenty-six downstairs.

One of the later RTs, seen here towards the end of its service life on route 140, which took red buses out as far as London's Heathrow Airport. This bus was typical of the RT class and wider RT family that served London for forty years.

Serviceable and elegant, the standard RT interior had been carefully thought out and wore exceptionally well in London conditions.

The RT was fundamentally an AEC design, but, Leyland were persuaded to modify their PD1 Titan chassis to suit London's standardised body. The RTL class were easily recognised by the absence of the triangular AEC badge on their radiator grilles. The visually similar Leyland RTWs were 8 feet wide instead of the 7 feet 6 inches of the RTs and RTLs.

The RT was an immediate success, and the LPTB ordered 150 more. However, the outbreak of war in 1939 delayed the arrival of the last examples until 1942, and then put a stop to RT production for five years. Ever optimistic, London Transport placed an order with AEC for more chassis in 1944, but the first of these were not delivered until 1947. Meanwhile, Chiswick had become so busy overhauling and repairing the existing fleet that the order for bodies had to be placed elsewhere. London stipulated that these bodies had to be built to a rigidly standardised design to permit full interchangeability.

Park Royal and Weymann received the body contracts, but materials shortages and demand from other customers meant that chassis production was soon running ahead of body production. So London Transport turned to two other companies to make up the shortfall. Saunders made bodies with detail differences from the standard design, but Craven merely adapted one of their standard types. Both were built in relatively small numbers.

There were problems with chassis production, too. When AEC was unable to keep up with demand, London Transport persuaded Leyland to make a 'Londonised' version of their PD1 chassis (called RTL-types in service), and subsequently a Londonised version of their new 8-foot-wide chassis (called RTWs). These introduced more body variations, and between 1949 and 1950 London's voracious demand for new buses had to be satisfied with a temporary class of SRTs, created by fitting new RT bodies to old STL chassis that had been overhauled and updated.

Although the RT body remained essentially unchanged until production ended in 1954, from 1948 the roof-mounted route number box (only at the front on post-war models) disappeared. These buses also carried a variety of different liveries as the amount of cream relative to the overall red was gradually reduced. Many were painted in the green of the country area fleet (see page 51).

There were 4,825 RTs, plus 1,631 RTLs and 500 RTWs. They formed the largest standardised bus fleet ever seen and became recognised worldwide as a symbol of London. The Leylands and non-standard body types were withdrawn first, but the last RTs remained in service until 1979 – four decades after the type had been introduced.

The RT family's two major tasks had been to replace London's worn-out pre-war bus fleet and then, from 1952, to finish replacing its trams whose withdrawal had begun in 1935. The Routemasters that followed also had two tasks: to replace London's trolleybus system from 1958, and then to replace the RTs themselves.

Planning for a new double-decker began in 1947. To save weight, it was to have a rigid aluminium body structure (inspired by Chiswick's wartime aircraft work) and no separate chassis; instead, the running units would be carried on demountable sub-frames. Once again, a very high degree of standardisation was required to simplify servicing and overhaul.

Led by Chiswick, the design came together with input from AEC and its associated bodybuilding company Park Royal. The first running prototype of the new Routemaster was ready in 1954 and, after trials with three more prototypes, RMs began to enter service in 1959.

London operating conditions still favoured a front-engine, rear-platform design, but these new buses were 18 inches longer than the RTs (at 27 feet 6 inches) and benefited from the new 8-foot width tested with the RTWs.

The first of the many: after four prototypes had been built, the first production Routemaster to be completed was given the fleet number RM8. The bus was retained at Chiswick for experimental purposes for most of its life and only ran briefly in service. It has now been preserved by a group of enthusiasts.

To meet new regulations governing overall length, later Routemasters were built with an extra half-bay in the middle of their bodies and an additional eight seats. This is one of the classified RML-types in central London near the Bank, displaying the later style of destination blind with yellow letters in place of white ones.

Careful juggling of space had given them a higher seating capacity of sixty-four (thirty-six upstairs, twenty-eight downstairs). Production models had AEC running-units, coil springs and independent front suspension for a better ride, and drivers appreciated their power hydraulic brakes, power-assisted steering and two-pedal semi-automatic transmission. Passengers also benefited from a proper heating and ventilating system.

The original hope was for some 4,000 Routemasters to be built to a standard design, but developments in the bus business conspired to make the RM class both less numerous – there were 2,760 in all – and ultimately rather less standardised than the RTs. All those built after 1965 were an extra 2 feet 6 inches long, and there were Green Line coach versions of both standard and long-wheelbase models. Some also had Leyland engines.

When it was new, the Routemaster embodied some advanced design features, but by the time the last was built in 1968, its design was quite old-fashioned. Double-deck bus design had largely moved over to front-entrance, rear-engined layouts, and these suited the growing demand for one-man operation. Nevertheless, the RM soldiered on in London service until 2005, and in the 1990s many buses were re-engined and refurbished to extend their lives, while others that had been withdrawn in favour of newer designs were put back into service.

In terms of its engineering, robustness, reliability and service life, the Routemaster is recognised as one of the best urban bus designs ever created. It is sad that developments in the bus business made its layout obsolete before its working life was over, and that changes in the ownership and management of London's buses made it the last London bus actually designed by London Transport.

So what made the RT and RM so widely loved, and why did they become such well-known symbols of London? To those who used them regularly, the standardised designs offered a reassuring familiarity, while careful use of colour inside created a light and spacious environment, which was both restrained and welcoming. Clever design of such items as radiused window corners eliminated dirt traps and added an indefinable air of quality, while the wide staircase and large rear platform with its conductor's well made these easy buses to use. There was also no doubt that the clean exterior lines had a certain friendliness in their gently rounded shapes that contrasted with the severe lines of so many contemporaries – and so many more recent designs.

Outside the UK, the RT and RM shapes also acquired a widespread familiarity. Between 1950 and 1975, London buses were regularly displayed as a symbol of London at overseas trade fairs, and invariably attracted great attention because they were so different from the local modes of transport. Members of the RT family went abroad on promotional duties eight times between 1950 and 1957, and Routemasters made no fewer than forty-one overseas promotional trips between 1961 and 1975. In this way, the red double-decker became more closely associated with London in the eyes of overseas tourists than ever before. Few publishers of London picture postcards subsequently failed to offer one with some red double-deckers visible, and few makers of mass-produced toy model buses failed to come up with a red London-type double-decker (even though strict accuracy was not always on the agenda).

The Red Rover ticket allowed unlimited travel on London's red buses at weekends. This 1982 example carries an image of an RML-type Routemaster bus.

Far left and opposite page: Two special 1951 Festival of Britain bus tickets.

Middle left: These punch-type tickets were issued in the early 1950s. The circular holes indicate where the passenger boarded the bus; the tear at the bottom of the penny ticket comes from the clip on the conductor's ticket rack.

Below: Two early Red Rover tickets.

THE CREWS

ALTHOUGH it took a vast army of people to keep London's buses running, the public's perception of London Transport staff was invariably limited to the ones they encountered on a day-to-day basis. In the period before one-man operation, there were three categories of these: drivers, conductors, and inspectors. The drivers drove; the conductors collected the fares; and the inspectors helped to ensure regularity of running, offered advice to passengers, and – most worryingly for many small boys – carried out random ticket checks on the buses.

Working on London's buses was seen as a respectable job in the period before the Second World War. It offered a high degree of job security and it provided operating crews and inspectors with a uniform – which was then seen as a mark of respectability in itself. The main disadvantage was that the hours could sometimes be unsociable.

However, from 1948 London Transport began to find it increasingly difficult to attract staff. Perhaps people's expectations in the post-war years were higher than they had been; perhaps the wearing of a uniform had become associated with military service and was something that many wished to forget; perhaps bus crews' pay no longer kept them in the 'respectable' bracket as far as society was concerned.

By 1956, the problem had become acute, and London Transport established a scheme for recruiting bus conductors (and some other menial jobs within both the bus and underground train divisions) directly from abroad. The scheme took off first in Barbados, which was then suffering from high unemployment. Its government offered to lend London Transport recruits their fares to the UK, and gradually crew strengths returned to workable levels.

The bus crews had their own trade union, too, and this showed its muscle as early as the late 1940s, during the discussions that led to the creation of the Routemaster bus. London Transport's early plan was to make the bus a seventy-seater, but the company backed down on this because they feared trouble with the union: conductors had been used to buses that carried no more than fifty-

Opposite:
Wartime necessities: while the menfolk were away fighting the war, women were recruited as conductresses ('clippies') to keep London's buses running. This picture was taken during the First World War and shows the white top coat of the summer uniform. Note the open staircase and the proliferation of advertisements on the bus, which had been built in 1912. (IWM Q 109768)

Before the days of front-entrance buses, drivers entered the cab with the aid of steps built into the bodywork. This 1947 London Transport poster shows a driver wearing a regulation-issue greatcoat and cap, and boarding his LT six-wheeler.

LT 617

LEO DOWD

AT YOUR SERVICE

One of the 22,000 drivers of the 9,500 London Transport road service vehicles which travel a total of 1,100,000 miles every day, carrying more than ten million passengers.

six passengers, and the jump to seventy would have added to their workload. So the first Routemasters compromised on just sixty-four seats.

By the late 1950s, the trade union had acquired even more influence, and over the summer of 1958 it called for a strike, demanding better pay and working conditions for London's bus crews. For the best part of two months, no buses ran in the capital and London's parks were turned into giant car parks to enable commuters to use their cars to get to work. It was a major turning point in London Transport's fortunes: more than 1,500 bus staff never returned to work but took up other employment, and London Transport estimated that 20 per cent of their passengers never returned to using the buses. The situation was compounded that October when the government made car purchase easier by abolishing hire purchase restrictions, and again some six months later when they reduced purchase tax.

Staff shortages remained a problem in the following decades. One solution, which many provincial operators had already embraced, was 'One Man Operation' (now known as 'One Person Operation'). Here, the driver collected the fares as passengers boarded the bus and there was no conductor at all. The system would only work if the passenger entrance was at the front of the bus, alongside the driver, and the traditional London double-decker with its rear entrance was ill suited to this. So, as the final chapter shows, from the mid-1960s the design of London's buses gradually changed to meet the new requirements.

TICKETS

The conductor's primary job was to ensure that every passenger on his or her bus had paid the appropriate fare. To this end, a ticket was issued as a

The Gibson ticket machine began to enter London service in 1953.

Samples of Gibson
tickets.

Opposite:
Getting a free
uniform still meant
something in 1954
when this
recruitment poster
was issued,
although London
Transport was
finding it
increasingly
difficult to attract
new staff. The bus
is an RT-type.

payment receipt. From an early date, tickets were printed in different colours to indicate their different 'values' in pennies, and conductors carried them in a neat wooden rack with spring clips. On each ticket was also pre-printed a list of the key stops along the route. The conductor carried a small punch that clipped a piece of the ticket out, indicating where the passenger had boarded. It was thus an easy job for an inspector, later on, to check whether a passenger had paid the correct fare or not.

Various types of punch were used until the 1950s, but from 1953 all were gradually replaced by the Gibson ticket machine, which allowed the conductor to print tickets as required on a paper roll. It was quicker and cheaper than the older methods. Green Line coaches used different machines. New ticket-issuing machines followed changes in London's fare structure in the 1990s, but not long afterwards, a new system was introduced to speed up the boarding process, and customers had to buy their tickets from a machine at the bus stop before they boarded the bus.

INSPECTORS

Although the jobs of the driver and conductor were more or less self-explanatory, that of the inspector was not. Many inspectors were former drivers or conductors who had done well and moved up the ranks: an inspector was better paid than the operating crew.

One of the inspector's two chief functions was to ensure that buses ran on time (and they were often seen recording the time at which certain buses – identified by a garage code on stencils or removable alloy plates – passed a given point). This involved overseeing the drivers, ensuring that they did not lose time on the route.

The inspector's other main function was to oversee the conductors, and they would board buses to check that all passengers had a ticket. Although this helped identify those who had travelled on further than they had paid for, it was also a way of checking that the conductor had done his or her job properly.

WOMEN CREWS

Traditionally, bus crews had always been male, but as men were conscripted into the armed forces during the First World War, London recruited its first women as conductors. These pioneers were given a special uniform and quickly acquired the nickname of 'clippies' because their job was to clip a portion from passengers' tickets. Although men took back most jobs on London's buses after the war was over, women staff gradually became more common and, as this was the period after emancipation, more tolerated socially.

Similar acute staff shortages came about as a result of the Second World War. London appointed Mrs Dorothy McKenzie as its first female bus driver

London Transport

needs

Men & Women

CONDUCTORS

- A regular job

- Free uniform

- Free travel on London Transport buses

- Good canteens and sports facilities

Apply to
The London Transport Recruitment Centre
Griffith House
280 Marylebone Road, N.W.I
Adjoining Edgware Rd. Station
      (Metropolitan Line)

All engagements are made in accordance with
The Notification of Vacancies Order 1952

in 1941, and she was followed by many more. The war years saw many female conductors, too, and although men reclaimed the drivers' jobs after the war, there were many female conductors ('conductresses') from at least the early 1950s.

It took many years for the female bus driver to return, though, and the appointment of Jill Viner as a London bus driver in 1974 was an occasion for comment in the national newspapers. Since then, female bus drivers have become less uncommon, and such things as power-assisted steering, brakes and gearchanges in modern buses have removed the last arguments that driving London's buses was strictly a man's job.

TRAINING

If the pay and social status of London's bus crews declined after 1945, the standards required from them did not. London Transport was always very proud of its staff training programmes, which were carried out primarily at its Chiswick operational headquarters.

Drivers, conductors and inspectors alike were put through rigorous training procedures in the basic functions of their jobs and also to ensure passenger safety. Drivers, for example, were taught on the famous skid-pan how to regain control of a skidding bus, while conductors were trained in such things as how to prevent a passenger from falling off the platform of a moving bus. None of that prevented passengers sometimes from trying to board a moving bus, and the author witnessed one nasty accident in which a passenger was dragged behind a bus. He grabbed the handrail but fell short of the platform as he jumped.

Drivers were licensed and wore a badge to advertise the fact. This one dates from 1907; horse-bus drivers had a badge that read 'Animal Power'.

UNIFORMS

For most of the first half of the twentieth century, London bus crews were proud of their uniforms. The first of these were probably those issued by the General in 1909, when it provided its drivers with caps and jackets. By 1912, knee-length greatcoats were available – probably a necessity in an open cab in the middle of winter!

As time went on, so the crews were issued with different uniforms for summer and winter. The winter issue was in dark blue serge, and each crew member had a badge carrying his or her personal staff number, which would be pinned to the lapel of the jacket. Drivers, conductors, and inspectors

STAGE DRIVER 1112 MECHANICAL POWER

A conductor in summer uniform, pictured with his Gibson ticket machine on the top deck of a Routemaster in 1976. By this time, most staff dispensed with caps, which were no longer compulsory wear.

alike had matching caps with a stiff peak. Summer uniforms included a white top cover for the cap and, for drivers, a long white top coat. During the Second World War, inspectors were issued with a white jerkin, which they wore over their dark blue uniforms so that they could be more easily seen in the blackout.

During the 1950s, conductors were also provided with a new summer uniform, which was distinguished by a grey cotton jacket in place of the blue serge 'winter' type. However, pride in uniforms began to dwindle in this period, and although bus crews are still issued with uniforms to this day, many now prefer to wear clothes of their own choosing, which only broadly fit in with the standards their employers expect.

SINGLE-DECKERS AND COUNTRY COUSINS

FROM the earliest days of the London motor bus, single-deckers were used on routes with either low passenger volumes or physical restrictions that ruled out double-deckers. There has also been a substantial fleet of green 'country area' buses and coaches, supplemented by both single- and double-decker vehicles for the Green Line express services.

The earliest of London's red single-deckers were about thirty built on the B-type chassis, but far more numerous were the T-class AEC Regals built from 1929 onwards. There were single-decker variants of the LT-class AEC Renown six-wheelers in the 1930s, plus a motley collection of non-standard types, many inherited from the independents absorbed by the LPTB in 1933.

All these were swept away in the early 1950s by the standardised RF class of front-entrance, underfloor-engined AEC Regal IVs. These remained London's standard single-deckers until the 1970s, some being converted for driver-only operation in their later years. Since then, lower passenger volumes and the focus on driver-only operation have brought a large number of proprietary single-decker types into the London fleet, beginning with the unsuccessful AEC Merlins and Swifts of the 1970s and leading on to the articulated Mercedes-Benz 'bendy buses' of the turn of the century.

Since 1912, the LGOC had operated a number of routes radiating out from the London metropolitan area, many in association with independents such as East Surrey Traction and the National Omnibus and Transport Company. As London's suburbs began their dramatic expansion in the 1920s, the need for such services increased, and two different types of bus service became established.

One was the stage-carriage service in the outer London area (defined by the 1924 London Traffic Act as more than 25 miles in any direction from Charing Cross), and the other was the longer-distance express coach service, typically crossing London from one side to another. Both took London buses out beyond the suburbs and into the counties surrounding the city – Hertfordshire in the north, Essex in the east, Kent and Surrey in the south, and Berkshire in the west.

Opposite: Successors to the front-engined T class were the RF class, built on underfloor-engined AEC Regal IV chassis. There were red buses for the central area, green buses for the country area, and Green Line coaches with different seating. This example had been adapted for one-man operation when pictured in the 1980s.

701 ASCOT VIA VIRGINIA WATER

704 BROMLEY SEVENOAKS TUNBRIDGE WELLS

710 AMERSHAM 710 CHESHAM SUNDAY

718 KINGSTON VICTORIA HARLOW FARE STAGE

Above:
Green Line services had their own bus-stop E-plates.

Left:
Now owned by the London Bus Preservation Trust, T31 is typical of the single-deckers of the 1930s used on the less well-patronised outer suburban routes. It was new to the LGOC in December 1929 on the recently introduced AEC Regal chassis.

The LGOC also tried examples of the pioneering AEC Q-type, with its engine mounted at the side behind the driver. These were advanced buses for the early 1930s, but neither they nor the double-deck AEC Qs were bought in large numbers. Some were used in the country area.

Left:
The longer distances covered by some country routes called for higher ticket values, like those seen here.

Right:
This Setright ticket was issued on a Green Line service in the early 1960s.

persuade London Transport of the need for double-decker coaches on some of the busier routes from 1962. Initially, these were variants of the ubiquitous Routemaster. However, the spread of suburban electric railway services and increases in private car ownership gradually undermined the viability of many Green Line services during the 1960s.

From 1 January 1970, both country-area and Green Line services passed into the hands of the National Bus Company and out of the hands of the London authority that had operated them for so long. The new London Country Bus Services took over the fleet of London-standard RT, RF and RM vehicles, but these gradually disappeared in favour of new buses. The dark green livery and London Transport fleet name also disappeared in favour of a lighter green and the London Country fleet name.

Further developments in the mid-1980s saw LCBS divided into four separate regional operating companies. Green Line went through a difficult period but retained its identity through changes of ownership, and by the turn of the century was operating services further out of London than ever before, as well as a network of airport-linking routes and fast motorway services.

In later years, Green Line express services expanded to provide airport links from central London. This Leyland Leopard from 1981 was running the 757 Flightlink service between the traditional Green Line terminus at Victoria's Eccleston Bridge and Luton Airport.

MODERN TIMES

Dwindling passenger numbers forced London Transport to develop new services in the 1970s and 1980s. The Red Arrow express routes offered rapid transit in busy parts of London's West End, where travel by car was next to impossible and Underground trains would take much longer. This poster dates from 1982.

T OWARDS THE END of the twentieth century, a combination of politics and changing demand for passenger services brought about the demise of the traditional London bus, as well as sweeping away the impressive standardisation of bus types which the LPTB and its LTE successor had fought so hard to achieve. London's bus services entered a period of decline and confusion from which they took a very long time to emerge.

Things began to change in the 1960s. Increases in private car usage were inexorably leading to falling passenger numbers and therefore to falling revenues, and outside London many bus operators had turned to one-man operation (OMO). Having the driver take the fares as passengers boarded the bus dispensed with the need for a conductor and so saved money, but with their front-engined, rear-entrance layout, the majority of London's double-deck buses could not be adapted to suit.

In a sense, London Transport was rushed into changing its operating practices. No new London bus intended for OMO was even in the design stages, but the need for one was pressing. So London compromised,

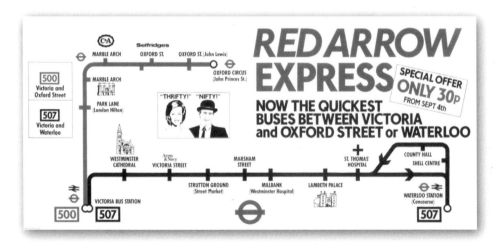

56

beginning in November 1964 by adapting front-entrance single-decker RFs for OMO use on outer London services and following up with a variety of new off-the-peg vehicles. Previous practice, since the X-types of 1909, had been for London to develop its own buses to meet its uniquely arduous operating conditions. Many of the new purchases over the next two decades demonstrated the wisdom of this practice when they proved disappointingly unreliable.

The year 1966 saw high-capacity OMO single-deckers introduced for some special 'Red Arrow' routes in the central area. The AEC Merlins, and later AEC Swifts, that were bought for these services were notoriously unreliable and were being withdrawn by 1973, although deliveries continued until 1981. Their replacements were mainly double-deckers. Variants of these AEC models also took over from the long-serving RF single-deckers that worked the 'red' outer London services.

The first OMO double-deckers did not appear until 1971, but London's first front-entrance, rear-engined vehicles arrived as early as November 1965. These XA-class Leyland Atlanteans were swiftly followed by XF-class

The Red Arrow services, all numbered in the 500 series, were run by high-capacity 'standee' single-deck AEC Swift buses. Their reliability was disappointing, and passengers baulked at standing up while travelling rather than sitting down. Several examples are seen in this 1970 scene at the important bus terminal outside Victoria Station.

London's earliest rear-engined double-deckers were not an unqualified success. This is a one-man-operated DMS-class Daimler Fleetline at Aldgate Underground station.

Daimler Fleetlines, and further experimental vehicles included a remarkable front-entrance, rear-engined double-decker called the FRM that was created from 80 per cent of standard Routemaster parts. However, the political climate was pushing London Transport towards accepting off-the-peg designs, and the problem of falling revenues was a further deterrent to investment in a new bespoke model.

Reliability issues blighted the career of the so-called 'Londoner' or DMS-class buses on Daimler Fleetline chassis in the 1970s, and their service life of less than ten years was a stark contrast to the three and four decades of the purpose-built RTs and RMs. By the middle of the decade, however, new and more reliable front-entrance, rear-engined double-deckers were arriving: MD-class Metro-Scanias, the further-developed M-class Metrobuses and the T-class Leyland Titans. These latter two were the last new double-deckers ordered by a united London Transport, because from 1984 politics brought about a fundamental change in the ownership of the capital's transport system.

When the GLC had passed responsibility for London's Country Area over to the National Bus Company in 1970, the London Transport fleet had immediately shrunk. This of course made the economics of developing a special bus design for London much less attractive. Then, with the change from a central operating authority to a series of smaller companies that began under LRT in 1984, the chances of large-scale standardisation returning to London's buses receded even further.

New fleet names appeared on the buses themselves, there were some new liveries, and bus types diversified even more. Although large-capacity double-deckers with front entrances and rear engines remained the staple format, different companies ordered different types, and not always from British manufacturers. After the turn of the millennium, Londoners became used to several varieties of low-floor double-deckers, designed to make boarding and alighting easier for handicapped and elderly passengers.

Dating from the mid-1980s is this LS-class Leyland National single-decker, built to a standardised pattern found all over the UK. As on so many buses of the period, passengers paid their fare on entry.

Above: As the 21st century opened, access for disabled and elderly passengers was given more careful consideration, and to this end the Volvo Wright Eclipse Gemini buses (VWLs to some operators and WVLs to others) had low entrance floors. The picture dates from 2007.

Below: Minibuses were increasingly used for routes with low passenger numbers. This MR-class bus was a one-man-operated MCW Metrorider with Cummins diesel engine and was new in 1988.

Many of these had attractively designed bodies, which were a far cry from the utilitarian styles of the early front-entrance, rear-engine double-deckers.

The single-deckers changed, too. By 1986, some areas had a new breed of twenty-five-seater bus whose small size matched reduced passenger demand and minimised operating costs. Early examples were Optare City Pacers, and these carried the Hoppa brand name because, in theory, it was easy to 'hop' onto one of these

The high-capacity articulated single-decker or 'bendy bus' of the early twenty-first century is represented by this EA-class Mercedes operated by First.

buses. More mini- and mid-sized single-deckers followed in the 1990s, and after 2003 some areas of the capital became home to large-capacity single-decker 'bendy buses'. These, based on Mercedes-Benz Citaro chassis, used an articulated design that was new to London but was already common in continental European cities.

By the end of the 1990s, investment in new types of bus and services that targeted passenger demands more effectively was at last beginning to improve the fortunes of London's buses. Bus use in the capital started to increase again after a long period of decline.

Yet the casual observer of London's buses in the early twenty-first century would probably not recognise how fundamentally the London bus landscape has changed. The buses in central London are still, by and large,

Typical of the modern London double-decker is this PVL-class Volvo President operated by London General. The bus was new in 2001.

Examples of tickets from 1987 and 1996 reflect the changing name of London's bus operating authority.

red double-deckers, even though the high degree of standardisation that once characterised the London fleet is no longer in evidence. Many of the single-deckers, red or otherwise painted, are smaller than their late-twentieth-century equivalents, but few people care very much as long as they run reliably. The only real controversy concerning the buses themselves has concerned the 'bendy buses', which were long enough to block junctions and were thought to pose a particular hazard to cyclists. In 2008, the then newly elected mayor of London, Boris Johnson, pledged to replace these vehicles with a 'new Routemaster'. If that happens, the story of London's bus standardisation could begin all over again.

The deregulation of bus services in the capital had some interesting consequences. In the 1980s and 1990s, bus dealer Ensignbus operated a network of routes in east London, and often ran them with preserved London Transport vehicles. Like this RT, they maintained their former livery but with the addition of an Ensignbus fleetname. The company still operates a historic fleet of around 20 former London buses.

FURTHER READING

Many books about London buses have been produced for the enthusiast market, but these are often short-run publications and quickly become hard to find except in specialist shops. The selection below is no more than representative of books on the subject.

Baker, Michael H. C. *London Transport Since 1963*. Ian Allan Publishing, Shepperton, 1997.

Banks, John (photography by G. H. F. Atkins). *London Transport*. The Prestige Series, Venture Publications, 2000.

Blacker, Ken. *RT: The Story of a London Bus*. Capital Transport, Harrow Weald, 1979.

Blacker, Ken. *Routemaster. Volume One, 1954–1969*. Capital Transport, Harrow Weald, 1991.

Booth, Gavin. *The British Motor Bus*. PRC, 1992 (reprint of 1977 original).

Brewster, D. E. *London General Buses*. Oakwood Press, Shaftesbury, 1984.

Curtis, Colin, and Townsin, Alan. *Chiswick Works*. Capital Transport, Harrow Weald, 2000.

Elborough, Travis. *The Bus We Loved: London's Affair with the Routemaster*. Granta Books, London, 2005.

Robbins, George. *General Buses of the Twenties: An Introduction to the K, S, NS, LS Classes*. Images Publishing, Malvern, 1996.

Townsin, Alan. *Blue Triangle*. The Transport Publishing Company, Glossop, 1980.

PLACES TO VISIT

London Bus Preservation Trust, Redhill Road, Cobham, Surrey KT11 1EF. Telephone: 01932 868665. Website: www.lbpt.org
Laid out more like a working bus garage than a museum, the LBPT's premises are home to around 35 old London buses. Many of the buses run local services on various days during the year, giving an unrivalled opportunity to ride on one of London's classic buses.

London Transport Museum, Covent Garden Piazza, London WC2E 7BB. Website: www.ltmuseum.co.uk
The museum is dedicated not only to London's buses but to every other form of public transport that has served the capital. The museum has an extensive archive collection as well as an excellent collection of buses, trams and trolleybuses on display.

INDEX

Page numbers in italic refer to illustrations.